For all of the NICU babies and families I have had the honor of caring for over the years.

NICU (Dad) Strong

Written by Rachel Bowman

Illustrated by Nayab Shaheen

I don't know if you could feel me, but I was there
Pacing back and forth,
Worrying,
Wishing I could take your place,
Longing for your mother to be
able to touch your face

2

It's a father's job to be able
to take away the pain
But I was helpless when you
arrived too early that day

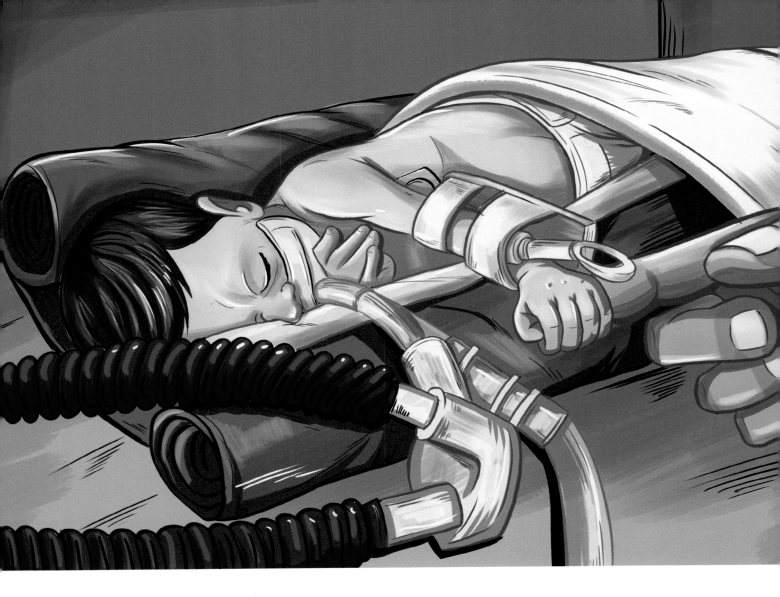

The doctors spoke about the
small chance of survival

But I saw your tiny fingers wrap
around those wires...

And I knew then you would be a fighter

I held your mama's hand,
as she held you
The first time after weeks
It's not something we imagined
having to wait to do

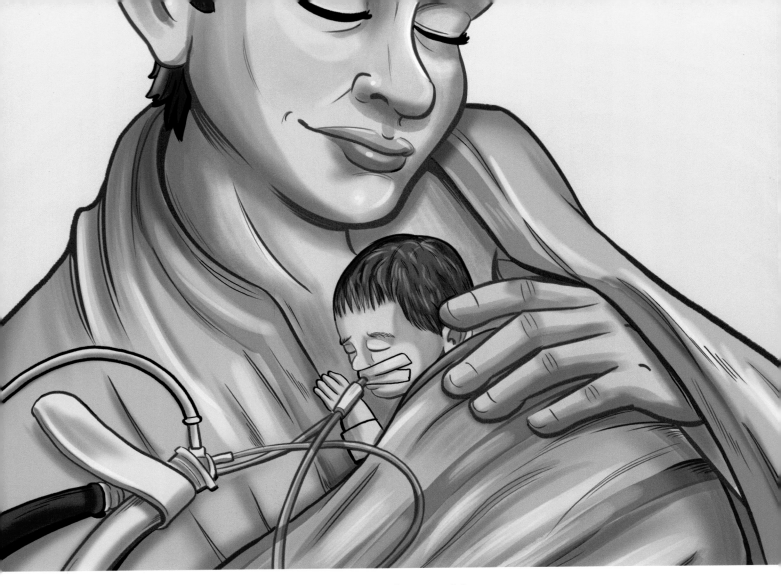

Two months in, and it was
my turn in the chair
They put us skin to skin for kangaroo care
I was intimidated by your tiny size
And your mama had to wipe
the tears from my eyes

At first, I didn't know what role to play

But I was taught that I could help
support you in many ways

There was touch and containment,

Diaper changes,

And reading for your brain development

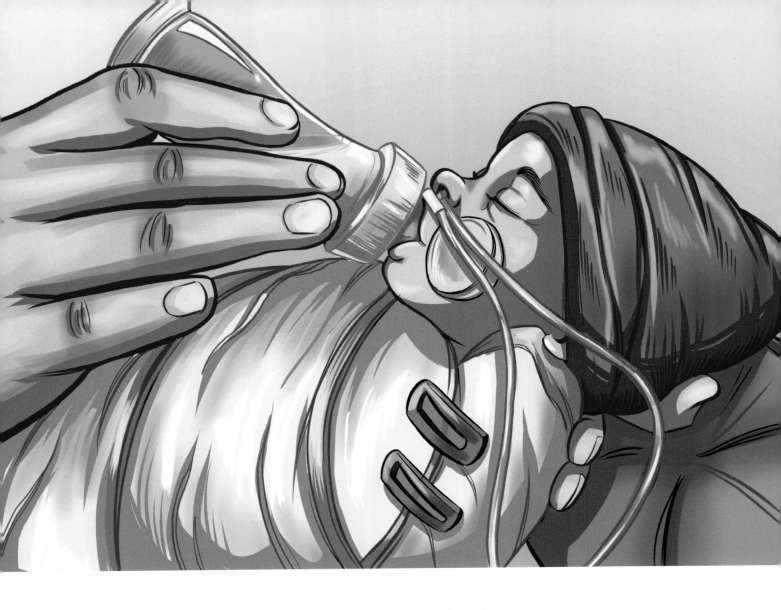

We fed you through tubes
And then the bottles came later
When you graduated to a
cannula from a ventilator

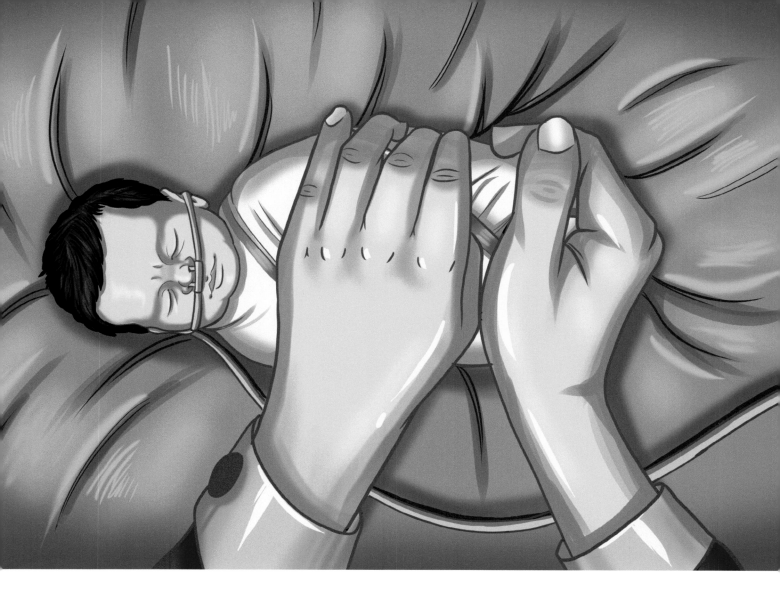

We rode the many NICU waves
Taking it slowly through the good and bad days
There were days of growth and progress
And the days we faced the occasional setbacks

I supported your growth and invested in mine
At times, I blamed myself for your occasional declines
So, when the anxiety made it too unbearable of a task
I sought help from a therapist

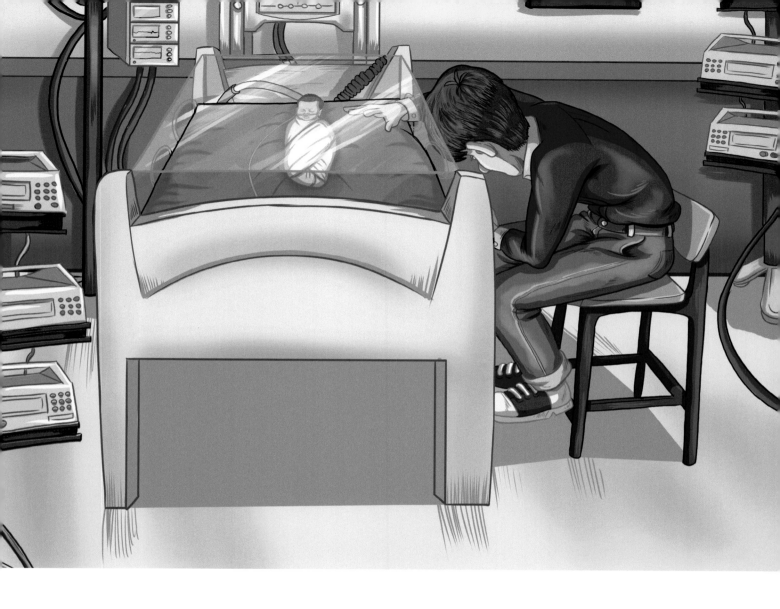

Child, I never left your side
Not through rain nor shine
Or the multiple, terrifying mountains
That seemed almost impossible to climb

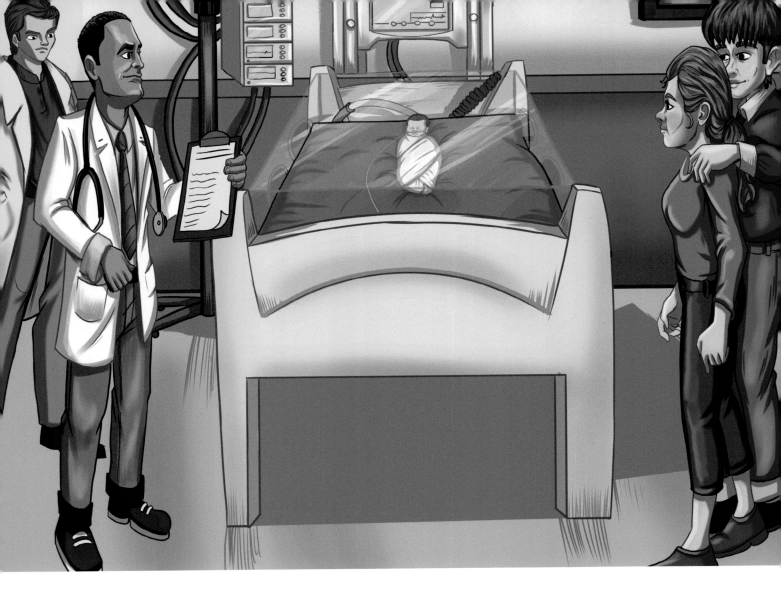

I learned to ask the important questions and advocate for you
It took me time to understand that I was a part of your treatment team too
At times, I felt stuck and scared
But with more education, I became better prepared

And then the big day came!
The doctors said you were strong enough to go home
You were drinking full bottles
And met all your discharge milestones

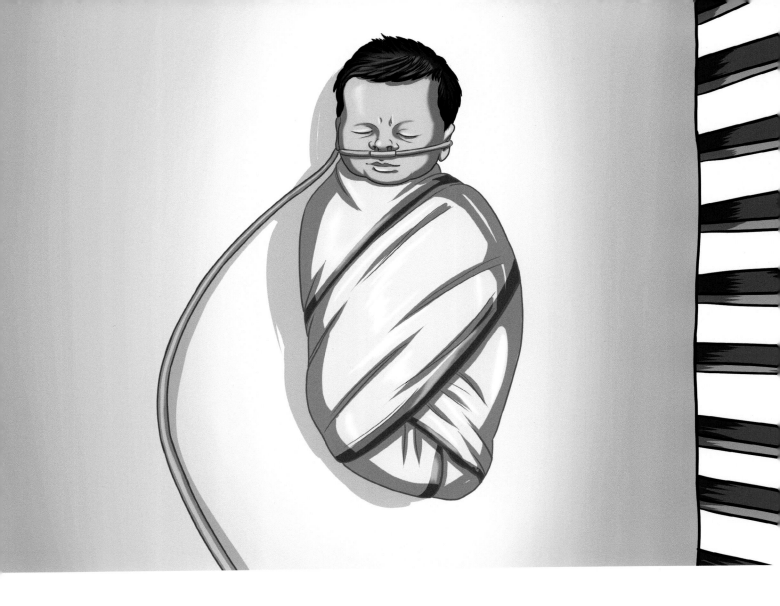

We set up for home oxygen
So, you could finally sleep in your nursery
The beeping of the machines up on the wall so high
No longer your nightly lullaby

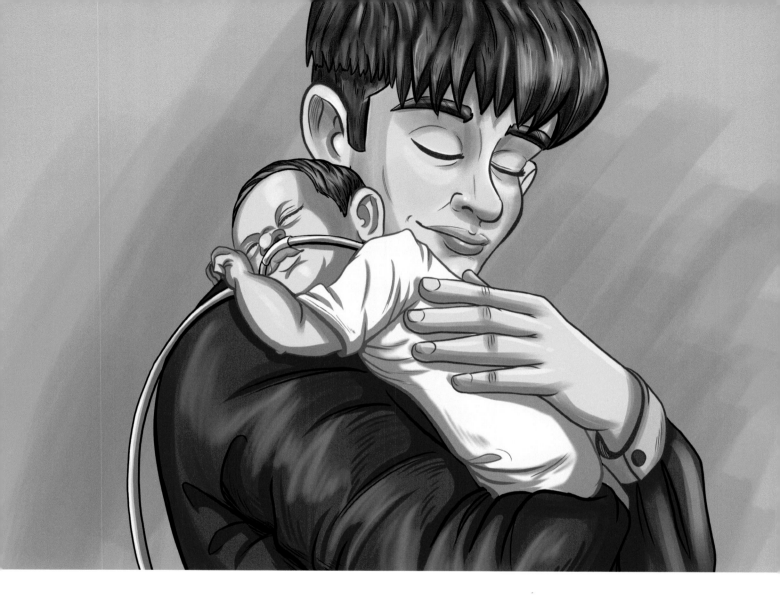

I'll keep watching you grow
And watching you thrive
We will look back on these days
With tears in our eyes

Because bravery isn't something you have to grow into
Our preemie taught us...
Strength is already inside of you!